Shredded WIT

Vern McLellan

HARVEST HOUSE PUBLISHERS
Eugene, Oregon 97402

Except where otherwise indicated, all Scripture verses in this book are taken from the Living Bible, copyright © 1971 by Tyndale House Publishers, Wheaton, Illinois. Used by permission.

SHREDDED WIT

Copyright © 1988 by Vern McLellan
Published by Harvest House Publishers
Eugene, Oregon 97402

ISBN 0-89081-629-8

Printed in the United States of America.

For more than a quarter of a century, I've been fortunate to have the skillful help of several capable secretarial assistants.

They have scrutinized, categorized, alphabetized, and typed thousands of one-liners for quick and easy reference.

To them I gratefully dedicate this book.

Bettye Blakley; Littleton, Colorado
Ann Polley; Sydney, Australia
Rosalyn Sutton; Rock Hill, South Carolina
Jean Elliott; Charlotte, North Carolina
Carol Sundberg; Fort Mill, South Carolina
Karen Gilchrist; Charlotte, North Carolina

Contents

Foreword

It is a great skill to be able to make people laugh so they can see things seriously. It is an art to marry ideas that are far apart with a flash of understanding and insight. True wit is the ability to perceive life as it is and express it in a humorous manner with an unexpected explosion of thought.

Vern McLellan is a connoisseur of proverbs and quotations that convey important thoughts for the common man. He, like the collector of gold coins, has put together a treasure chest of wisdom couched in humor and filled with insight. His other collections include: *Quips, Quotes and Quests*; *Proverbs for People*; and *Proverbs, Promises, and Principles*. In his latest book, *Shredded Wit*, he has included many humorous and serious proverbs and quotes that carry a very powerful punch of reality.

The Bible tells us that a cheerful heart is like a medicine—it is good for the soul. It is healthy to smile. In fact, I would take an ounce of wit to a pound of sorrow any day. You see, a sense of humor can help us overlook the unattractive. Humor helps us to be tolerant of the unpleasant. Humor helps us to cope with the unexpected and smile through the unbearable. It has been said, "A sense of humor is like a pole that adds balance to our steps as we walk the tightrope of life."

A good proverb is like salt in the conversation. It adds flavor. One must be reminded, however, that too much salt destroys the meal. There is a balance between wit, which burns bright, and judgment, which gives durable heat. Together they make the best fire. As Spurgeon, the great preacher, said, "The joking of wits, like the playing of puppies, often ends in snarling. . . . Wit without discretion is a sword in the hand of a fool."

I hope that you will enjoy the wisdom, humor, and nourishment of *Shredded Wit*, as I have. Thank you, Vern, for giving us added insight and laughter as we have looked at the truth of life. When I begin to think that I'm filled with great wit, I am brought back to the truth that I'm usually half right.

—Bob Phillips
Fresno, California

A Word from the Author

In *Shredded Wit*, we've quipped, snipped, snapped, popped, crackled, punned, and joked about breakfast foods and their next of kin.

Though millions skip breakfast, the experts assert that children need to eat more often than adults to maintain their energy levels and powers of concentration during the morning class lessons. For children and adults alike, a good breakfast meets about one-fourth to one-third of the day's total nutritional requirements.

In the business world, the "power breakfast" is replacing the long business lunch. *Washington Post* writers Jean Meyer and Jeanne Goldberg suggest: "From a nutritional point of view, there is no reason why some foods are considered breakfast fare and others are rarely eaten in the morning. But, most Americans have a well-defined view of breakfast foods, and few find pleasure in tuna or a turkey leg in the morning.

"Given that, we suggest a morning menu along these lines: orange juice, or another 100 percent fruit juice rich in vitamin C; hot or cold, low-sugar cereal with skimmed or low-fat milk; and tea or coffee, if you wish. A dish of low-fat yogurt with sliced fresh fruit and a slice of whole grain toast make another excellent choice. So does low-fat mozzarella cheese melted on whole grain toast, again with a good source of vitamin C, such as half a grapefruit or a dish of sliced strawberries."

So give yourself a break—eat a hearty breakfast! Before you head for your fast lane, load up on vitamins and minerals and other key ingredients to give your day a good start.

While you're taking care of the physical side of life, take a few meditative moments before you tune in the morning news and commentary. As the psalmist said, "Each morning I will look to you in heaven and lay my requests before you, praying earnestly" (Psalm 5:3). Your day will go much better if you take time first thing in the morning to tune up and harmonize. Enjoy some practical, plain vanilla Bible verses, devotional music, inspirational cassettes and significant prayer, and you'll be on your way to a beautiful day.

For your recommended daily allowance of inspirational one-liners, try a bowlful of *Shredded Wit*. These powerful, provocative, penetrating points will brighten your day, sharpen your wit, and quicken your step.

Solomon, the wisest man who ever lived, said, "I want those already wise to become the wiser and become leaders by exploring the depths of meaning in these nuggets of truth. How does a man become wise? The first step is to trust and reverence the Lord!" (Proverbs 1:5-7).

Also, before you slip into sleep, take a spoon-size dose of *Shredded Wit*. You'll slide into slumber with a smile on your face and a warm feeling in your heart.

I hope I've been able to whet your wit buds a bit.

—Vern McLellan
Charlotte, North Carolina

Shredded
WIT

Kix

He who kicks up a storm should expect rough sailing.

* * *

People who do things for kicks should expect kickbacks.

* * *

He who pulls on the oars doesn't have time to rock the boat.

* * *

Putting your best foot forward doesn't mean to kick about everything.

* * *

A mule makes no headway when he is kicking; neither does a man.

* * *

He who beefs too much winds up in a stew.

The person who is always finding fault seldom finds anything else.

*   *   *

Even after they come in, some people keep on knocking.

*   *   *

When looking for faults, use a mirror, not a telescope!

*   *   *

Those who complain about the way the ball bounces are often the ones who dropped it.

*   *   *

"Whines" are the products of sour grapes.

*   *   *

Over a rack of umbrellas: Don't frown at the rain— it's the only thing coming down.

*   *   *

If you growl all day, it's only natural you'll feel dog-tired at night.

The trouble with being a grouch is that you have to make new friends every few months.

*   *   *

A rebel doesn't care about the facts. All he wants to do is yell (Proverbs 18:2).

*   *   *

A grouch spreads cheer wherever he doesn't go.

*   *   *

Critics: People who go places and boo things.

*   *   *

Have you ever noticed that most knocking is done by folks who don't know how to ring the bell?

*   *   *

Bernard Baruch once reminded us that two things are bad for the heart—running up stairs and running down people.

*   *   *

The deadline for all complaints was yesterday!

*   *   *

If you can't stand the heat, stay out of the kitchen.

An honest critic helps to preserve freedom. But the man who constantly criticizes without checking his facts is a threat to freedom.

*   *   *

The trouble with most of us is that we would rather be ruined by praise than saved by constructive criticism.

*   *   *

If what they are saying about you is true, mend your ways. If it isn't true, forget it and go about your business.

Special K

Kindness

I shall pass this way but once; any good thing therefore that I can do, or any kindness that I can show, let me do it now. Let me not defer it or neglect it for I shall not pass this way again.

* * *

He who grows roses in his garden also does a kindness to his neighbors.

* * *

Nothing gives a person greater pleasure than doing a good deed in secret and having it found out by accident.

* * *

Don't expect to enjoy the cream of life if you keep your milk of human kindness all bottled up.

* * *

Kindness is one of the most difficult things to give away. It is usually returned.

When somebody does a man a favor, right away he's anxious to return it—which is quite all right. However, isn't it better to pass that favor along—to the next man who needs it? It seems that favors are meant to pass along—not just to return.

*   *   *

If someone were to pay you ten cents for every kind word you ever spoke about people, and collect for every unkind word, would you be rich or poor?

*   *   *

Kindness is simply loving people more than they deserve.

*   *   *

Money will buy a fine dog, but only kindness will make him wag his tail.

*   *   *

The person who sows seeds of kindness enjoys a perpetual harvest.

*   *   *

Better a little kindness while living than an extravagant floral display at the funeral.

*   *   *

Kindness is a language which the deaf can hear and the blind can see.

Be kind to everybody. You never know who might show up on the jury at your trial.

* * *

A kind word picks up a man when trouble weighs him down.

Kneeling

Seven days without prayer makes one weak.

* * *

If your knees are knocking, kneel on them.

* * *

Chin up, knees down.

* * *

The quickest way to get back on your feet is to get down on your knees.

* * *

You're on your toes when you're on your knees.

* * *

He stands best who kneels most; he stands strongest who kneels weakest; he stands longest who kneels lowest. Bent knees make strong backs.

Many a man kept going straight because his mother bent her knees in prayer.

*   *   *

He who is swept off his feet needs to get back on his knees.

*   *   *

Prayer is the stop that keeps you going.

*   *   *

You will never stumble if you stay on your knees.

*   *   *

The Lord . . . delights in the prayers of his people (Proverbs 15:8).

*   *   *

I have been driven many times to my knees, by the overwhelming conviction that I had nowhere else to go. My own wisdom and that of all those about me seemed insufficient for that day—*Abraham Lincoln*.

Knowledge

We have learned to swim under the water like fish; we have learned to fly through the air like birds; all we now have to do is learn to walk this earth like men.

Some students drink at the fountain of knowledge—others just gargle.

*   *   *

If you want to get into *Who's Who*, you had better first learn what's what.

*   *   *

Conceit is what makes a little squirt think he's a fountain of knowledge.

*   *   *

The fellow who knows more than his boss should be careful to conceal it.

*   *   *

No one is ever too old to learn, but many people keep putting it off anyway.

*   *   *

No God, no peace; know God, know peace.

*   *   *

Father to teenage son: Maybe you should start shifting for yourself now while you still know everything.

Lucky Charms

A visitor to Las Vegas was so unlucky he lost his shirt in a coin laundry.

*   *   *

A rabbit's foot is a poor substitute for horse sense.

*   *   *

Too many people get their exercise by jumping to conclusions, running up bills, stretching the truth, bending over backward, lying down on the job, side-stepping responsibility, and pushing their luck.

*   *   *

There may be luck in getting a job but there's no luck involved in keeping it.

*   *   *

The harder you work, the luckier you get—*Gary Player*.

People who wait upon fortune are never sure of dinner.

*   *   *

A man who depends on the breaks to win usually goes broke.

*   *   *

It is better to get your hands dirty—and eat, than to be too proud to work—and starve (Proverbs 12:9).

*   *   *

He who wants to make a splash in the puddle of life must be willing to jump.

*   *   *

People who trust all things to chance make a lottery of their lives.

*   *   *

Good luck often has the odor of perspiration about it.

*   *   *

Did you hear about the man who was so lazy he stuck his nose outside so the wind could blow it?

The man who is waiting for something to turn up might do well to start with his own shirt-sleeves.

* * *

How many fashion their lives after french bread—one long loaf!

* * *

Too many people are ready to carry the stool when the piano needs to be moved.

* * *

The only place where success comes before work is in the dictionary.

* * *

Boss to employee: You're a good man, Remington—punctual, industrious, efficient, pleasant, and loyal. You're also making the other employees very, very nervous.

* * *

Even a mosquito doesn't get a slap on the back until he starts to work.

* * *

The more steam you put into your work, the louder you can whistle when the work is done.

Some people remind us of blisters. They don't show up until the work is done.

* * *

People who believe that the dead never come back to life should be here at quitting time.

* * *

Oscar Hammerstein once said, "The difference between an amateur and a professional is this: An amateur hopes; a professional works."

* * *

"Son," said the tactful boss to the lazy office boy, "I don't know how we're going to get along without you, but starting Monday, we're going to try."

* * *

The man who watches the clock will always be one of the hands.

Wit Chex

Now is the time for all men to do spot checks—in thoughts, words, and action.

        *   *   *

The brain is no stronger than its weakest think. That's why a check-up from the neck-up is important.

        *   *   *

The brain is a powerful mechanism. It equals ten Empire State buildings in size. All of the water of the Niagara River is necessary to cool it and operate it.

        *   *   *

You aren't what you think you are; what you think you are!

        *   *   *

It's unfortunate that rusty brains do not squeak.

The most underdeveloped territory in the world lies under your hat.

* * *

If there is a substitute for brains it has to be silence.

* * *

Use your brain. It's the little things that count.

* * *

Your brain becomes a mind when it's fortified with knowledge.

* * *

I use not only all the brains I have, but all I can borrow—*Woodrow Wilson*.

* * *

One morning, every office at IBM headquarters bore the now-famous admonition on one of its walls:

THINK

The next morning the executives arrived to find, beneath the sign, this addition:

OR THWIM

Be sure your brain is in gear before you engage your mouth.

*   *   *

As soon as you open your mouth, your mind is on parade.

*   *   *

The mouths of many people seem to have the habit of going on active duty while their brains are on furlough.

*   *   *

The best way to save face is to keep the lower part shut.

*   *   *

Profanity is an evidence of the lack of sufficient vocabulary—and brains!

*   *   *

The human tongue is only a few inches from the brain, but they seem miles apart when some people talk.

*   *   *

Watch your thoughts for they may break out into words in a moment's notice.

Don't forget that people will judge you by your actions, not your intentions. You may have a heart of gold—but so does a hard-boiled egg.

*   *   *

People may doubt what you say, but they will always believe what you do.

*   *   *

Every action of our lives touches some chord that will vibrate in eternity.

*   *   *

The actions of men are the best interpreters of their thoughts.

*   *   *

He who has an abundance of push gets along very well without pull.

*   *   *

Too many people shoot blanks when aiming at their goals.

*   *   *

For success, try aspiration, inspiration, and perspiration.

Acting without thinking is a lot like shooting
without aiming.

*   *   *

Work brings profit; talk brings poverty!
(Proverbs 14:23).

Wild Oats

The favorite cereal of juvenile delinquents is "Wild Oats."

* * *

The price of wheat, wool, and corn goes up and down, but the price of wild oats stays the same.

* * *

When a youth begins to sow wild oats, it's time for father to start the threshing machine.

* * *

Life for some people is to sow wild oats during the week, and then go to church on Sunday and pray for a crop failure.

* * *

Wild oats take something out of the soil of a man's life that no system of crop rotation can restore.

Wild oats need no fertilizer.

*   *   *

Tim: Where was your brother going with that bag of oats?

Jim: Taking his girl out to dinner. He says she eats like a horse.

*   *   *

They strolled down the lane together,
  The sky was studded with stars.
They reached the gate in silence,
  And he lifted up the bars.

She neither smiled nor thanked him,
  For indeed she knew not how.
For he was just a farmer boy,
  And she—a jersey cow.

Fruity Pebbles

People who want to move mountains must start by carrying away small pebbles.

*   *   *

Success is not measured by height attained, but by obstacles overcome.

*   *   *

Sign in shop: The difficult we will do right away. The impossible takes us a little longer.

*   *   *

Challenge is the core and mainspring of all human activity. If there is an ocean, we cross it; If there is a disease, we cure it; If there is a wrong, we right it; If there is a record, we break it; and finally, if there is a mountain, we climb it.

*   *   *

You do not test the resources of God until you attempt the impossible—*F. B. Meyer*.

Schoolteacher: Johnny, can you tell me the difference between perseverance and obstinacy?

Johnny: One is a strong will, and the other is a strong won't.

*   *   *

Did you hear about the man who said, "I'm stubborn only when I don't get my own way"?

*   *   *

He who never changes his mind is either perfect to begin with or stubborn forever after.

*   *   *

It is senseless to pay tuition to educate a rebel who has no heart for truth; a rebellious son is a grief to his father and a bitter blow to his mother (Proverbs 17:16,25).

*   *   *

Don't waste your breath on a rebel. He will despise the wisest advice (Proverbs 23:9).

Team Flakes

Cooperation and teamwork will solve many problems. Even freckles make a nice coat of tan when they all get together!

*   *   *

Act like a heel toward teammates and you'll get walked on.

*   *   *

Cooperation determines the rate of progress.

*   *   *

Three fellows went to church and when it came time to pass the plate, the three discovered they had no money. Not wanting to be embarrassed, one fainted and the other two carried him out.

*   *   *

One lights the fire, the other fans it.

If you ever see a turtle on a stump, you know he didn't get there by himself.

* * *

Cooperate! Remember the banana. Every time it leaves the bunch, it gets skinned.

* * *

A man brought his elderly father to a psychiatrist. "I'm worried, Doc," he said. "My father has a junk wagon, and his horse's name is Joe. But he's getting confused. He'll drive the poor horse down the street and say, 'Come on, Joe! Come on, Steve! Come on, Sam!' "

The psychiatrist said to the junkman, "Your son says the horse's name is Joe."

The old man nodded. "Certainly it's Joe, but if he thought he was pulling the wagon all by himself, he'd have quit long ago"—*Kenneth E. Hall*.

* * *

One hand cannot applaud.

* * *

How wonderful it is, how pleasant, when brothers live in harmony! (Psalm 133:1).

At the staff meeting, the office manager said: All those disagreeing with me signify by saying "I quit."

* * *

A little boy was playing all alone in the front yard when a neighbor came along and asked where his brother was. "Oh," he said, "he's in the house playing a duet. I finished first."

* * *

A man was driving an auto with his wife in the back seat and stalled his car on the railroad tracks as the train was approaching. His wife screamed, "Go on! Go on!"

"You've been driving all day from the back seat. I've got my end across . . . now see what you can do with your end."

* * *

It's easy to get the players. Gettin' 'em to play together, that's the hard part—*Casey Stengel*.

Snap, Crackle, and Poppin' Off

So many people are like buttons—always popping off at the wrong time.

*   *   *

People who fly into a rage always make a bad landing.

*   *   *

Your life is in the hands of any person who makes you lose your temper.

*   *   *

About the time a man gets his temper under control, he goes out and plays golf again.

*   *   *

Nothing will cook your goose faster than a red-hot temper.

*   *   *

You don't get rid of your temper when you lose it.

Your temper may get you into trouble, but it is your pride that keeps you there.

*　　*　　*

He who loses his head usually is the last one to miss it.

*　　*　　*

Strike when the iron is hot—not when the head is hot.

*　　*　　*

People who are always hitting the ceiling are apt to be full of hot air.

*　　*　　*

He who is always blowing a fuse is usually in the dark.

*　　*　　*

People who have an ax to grind often fly off the handle.

*　　*　　*

For every minute you are angry, you lose 60 seconds of happiness.

He who has a sharp tongue soon cuts his own throat.

*   *   *

The greatest remedy for anger is delay.

*   *   *

When angry, count to ten before you speak; if very angry, count to 100—*Thomas Jefferson*.

*   *   *

Anger is the wind that blows out the lamp of intelligence.

*   *   *

Anger is just one letter short of danger.

*   *   *

Keep your mouth closed and you'll stay out of trouble.

*   *   *

A rebel shouts in anger; a wise man holds his temper in and cools it (Proverbs 29:11).

*   *   *

Never pick a quarrel—even when it's ripe.

If you speak when you're angry, you'll make the best speech you'll ever regret.

*   *   *

Husband during quarrel: You talk like an idiot.

Wife: I have to talk this way so you'll understand me.

*   *   *

Very often a fight for what is right turns into a quarrel for what is left.

*   *   *

Perhaps the only way to avoid quarreling with your wife is to let her go her way and you go hers.

*   *   *

It is hard to stop a quarrel once it starts, so don't let it begin (Proverbs 17:14).

*   *   *

There are usually two sides to every argument but no end.

*   *   *

People, like pins, are useless when they lose their heads.

Arguments provide plenty of heat but little light.
Actually, my wife and I are very romantic. We
won't even argue except by candlelight.

*   *   *

When arguing with a stupid person, be sure he isn't
doing the same thing.

*   *   *

Whether it's on the road or in an argument, when
the color changes to red, *Stop!*

*   *   *

It doesn't do to do much talking,
    When you're mad enough to choke,
For the word that hits the hardest,
    Is the one that's never spoke.
Let the other fellow do the talking,
    Till the storm has rolled away.
Then he'll do a heap of thinking,
    'Bout the things you didn't say.

*   *   *

The best time to keep your shirt on is when you're
hot under the collar.

*   *   *

He who "blows his stack" adds to the world's
pollution.

Puffed Wit

Don't brag, puff, and blow; it isn't the whistle that pulls the train.

*   *   *

There never was a person with an inflated ego who wasn't full of hot air.

*   *   *

When a man gets too big for his "britches," his hat doesn't fit either.

*   *   *

She who sings her own praise is usually off-key.

*   *   *

The man who falls in love with himself will have no competition.

*   *   *

A man who praises himself can drown in a thimbleful of water.

An egotist is a self-made man who's in love with his creator.

*   *   *

He who claims to be a self-made man has relieved God of an embarrassing responsibility.

*   *   *

People who are carried away by their own importance seldom have far to walk back.

*   *   *

The person who is all wrapped up in himself is overdressed.

*   *   *

Egotism: "I" strain.

*   *   *

Don't brag about your plan for tomorrow—wait and see what happens.

*   *   *

Don't praise yourself; let others do it! (Proverbs 27:2).

*   *   *

The best remedy for puffed-up pride is a pinprick.

Humility is a strange thing; the moment you think you have it, you have lost it.

Another Bran of Puffs

I owe a lot to smoking. Thanks to smoking, I now puff on cigarettes, cigars, pipes, and stairs.

* * *

Ashes to ashes and dust to dust—if cigarettes don't get you, the fallout must.

* * *

Misery is being a smoker—and being chased by a mugger who isn't.

* * *

Smoking: A fire at one end and a sucker at the other.

* * *

Smoker: Thank-you for holding your breath while I smoke.

* * *

Nonsmoker: I don't mind if you smoke here, but please don't exhale!

Did you hear about the man who read that smoking was bad for his health? He immediately gave up reading.

*　　*　　*

Many who are smoking more now are affording it less.

*　　*　　*

It's about the easiest thing in the world to give up smoking. I know one person who has done it a hundred times.

*　　*　　*

"Will my smoking this cigar bother you?"

"Not if my getting sick won't bother you!"

*　　*　　*

"Would you like a cigarette?"

"No thank-you. I think I already have cancer!"

*　　*　　*

Cancer cures smoking.

*　　*　　*

I don't smoke but I chew. Don't blow your smoke on me, and I won't spit on you.

Did you hear the latest report? Latest clinical tests prove more doctors smoke than camels.

* * *

To cigarette smokers: You pay twice for your cigarettes; once when you get them and once when they get you.

* * *

In the waiting room of a medical clinic in Chester, Vermont: To avoid holes in our carpet and your lungs, please refrain from smoking.

* * *

Sign in the dentist's office: Thanks for not smoking. We'd rather die of natural causes.

* * *

Nicotine is an awful curse; it strains the heart and drains the purse.

* * *

Question: What is the best way to stop someone from smoking?

Answer: Light their cigarette on both ends.

Breakfast of Chumps and Champs

Chumps have an itch for success but they're not willing to scratch for it.

*   *   *

Chumps stay awake nights figuring out how to succeed when they should have stayed awake days.

*   *   *

Chumps have the right aim in life but they've run out of ammunition.

*   *   *

Most failures are experts at making excuses.

*   *   *

The train of failure usually runs on the track of laziness.

*   *   *

Many of life's failures are men who did not realize how close they were to success when they gave up.

People who stop at third base to congratulate themselves will never score a home run.

*   *   *

Failure is the path of least persistence.

*   *   *

The greatest glory of men is not in never failing but in rising every time they fall.

*   *   *

A college boy sent home a telegram saying, "Mom! Have failed everything, prepare Pop!"

The reply came the next day, "Pop prepared . . . prepare yourself!"

*   *   *

In great attempts it is magnificent even to fail.

*   *   *

Winners find ways to make things work. Losers find excuses why things don't work.

*   *   *

Success comes in cans; failure comes in can'ts.

The road to success is always under construction.
Winning isn't everything, but wanting to win is—
Arnold Palmer.

*   *   *

God gave us two ends—one to think with and one
to sit on. Your success depends on which one you
use most.

*   *   *

A successful man is one who can lay a firm
foundation with the bricks others throw at him—
David Brinkley.

*   *   *

Isn't it amazing how quickly in life we credit our
setbacks to "bad luck" and our successes to "hard
work"?

*   *   *

Success is sweet, but its secret is sweat.

*   *   *

Winners are people who aren't afraid to take a
chance now and then. Losers sit around and wait
for the odds to improve.

He started to sing as he tackled the thing that couldn't be done, and he did it—*Edgar Guest*.

* * *

Do your best. Good is the enemy of best.

* * *

If you won't plow in the cold, you won't eat at the harvest (Proverbs 20:4).

* * *

Roadside sign in Kentucky: Pray for a good harvest, but keep on hoeing.

Greatnut Flakes

Thousands of nuts hold a car together but one nut can scatter it all over the road.

*   *   *

He who weaves through traffic may wind up in stitches.

*   *   *

Drive to arrive alive. It would be better to be a little late down here than too early up there.

*   *   *

The Sunday school teacher was describing how Lot's wife looked back and suddenly turned into a pillar of salt.

"My mother looked back once while she was driving," contributed little Johnny, "and she turned into a telephone pole."

*   *   *

Seatbelts are not as confining as wheelchairs.

Speed demons who drive too fast into the next county often wind up in the next world.

*   *   *

If your children want to take driving lessons, don't stand in their way.

*   *   *

Always try to drive so that your license will expire before you do. Drive carefully, and don't insist on your rites.

*   *   *

Seatbelts may be uncomfortable, but have you tried stretchers?

*   *   *

One way to make people slow down in their driving would be to call it work.

*   *   *

A lady was driving the wrong way down a one-way street when an officer stopped her: "Lady, didn't you see the arrow?"

"Sir, I didn't even see the Indians."

*   *   *

Drive sensibly. If you don't, your present car may last you a lifetime.

Famous last words: I wonder how much this car will do?

*   *   *

Conducting a funeral service, a Southern preacher eulogized: The shell's here, but the nut's gone.

*   *   *

He who wants to eat the kernel must first crack the nut.

*   *   *

Show me a squirrel's home, and I'll show you a nutcracker's suite.

*   *   *

Problems, like nuts, are sometimes hard to crack. The first step toward solving a problem is to see it clearly.

*   *   *

God has no problems—only plans—*Corrie ten Boom.*

*   *   *

Why can't problems hit us when we are 17 and know everything?

For every problem God permits us to have there is a solution—*Thomas Edison*.

* * *

Every problem is a possibility in disguise.

* * *

Be thankful for your problems. For if they were less difficult, someone with less ability would have your job.

* * *

Did you hear about the announcer who followed the pastor's radio sermon on "The Bread of Life" with these words: "This is the mutual bread-casting nutwork . . ."?

Nuts 'n' Honey

Wisdom is the main pursuit of sensible men, but a fool's goals are at the ends of the earth! (Proverbs 17:24).

*   *   *

A lot of trouble has been caused in the world by too much intelligence and too little wisdom.

*   *   *

Wisdom is what to do with what you know.

*   *   *

As a man grows wiser, he talks less and says more.

*   *   *

The wisest man remembers that to catch a mouse you starve a cat.

*   *   *

The door to wisdom swings on hinges of common sense and uncommon thoughts—*William A. Ward*.

A wise man is like a pin. His head keeps him from going too far.

* * *

A wise man is like a tack—sharp and pointed in the right direction.

* * *

Intelligence: Spotting a flaw in the boss' character.

Wisdom: Not mentioning it.

* * *

Wise people sometimes change their minds—fools, never.

* * *

It is generally agreed that some people are wise and some otherwise.

* * *

A wise man never plants more garden than his wife can hoe.

* * *

A wise man learns by the experience of others. An ordinary man learns by his own experience. A fool learns by nobody's experience.

God, grant me the serenity to accept the things I cannot change; the courage to change the things I can; and wisdom to know the difference—*Reinhold Niebuhr*.

* * *

Thinking well is wise; planning well wiser; doing well wisest of all.

* * *

He who is a wise man by day is no fool by night.

* * *

If wisdom's ways, you'd wisely seek
   Five things observe with care . . .
Of whom you speak, to whom you speak,
   And how, and why, and where.

* * *

Wisdom teeth are what develop when you bite off more than you can chew.

* * *

He is no fool who gives up what he cannot keep to gain what he cannot lose—*Jim Elliot*.

Life

Life is like a band—we need not all play the same part, but we must play in harmony.

* * *

Live your life, don't spend it.

* * *

Life is too short to wear a long face.

* * *

Don't get so busy making a living that you fail to make a life.

* * *

Don't take life so seriously—you won't get out of it alive!

* * *

The life of man: school tablet, aspirin tablet, stone tablet.

Life is like playing a violin solo in public and learning the instrument as one goes on.

* * *

Too many people will not throw away life at one time, but they will throw away a little of it each day.

* * *

The length of your life is less important than its breadth and depth.

* * *

Life does to us what life finds in us.

* * *

Remember, life is not made up of months and years. It is made up of hours, minutes, and seconds.

* * *

The trouble with life, you're halfway through before you realize it's one of those do-it-yourself deals.

* * *

Let us endeavor to so live that when we come to die, even the undertaker will be sorry—*Mark Twain*.

Did you hear about the undertaker who signed his letters, "Eventually yours"?

* * *

On the brevity of life: Man's a vapor and full of woes, he cuts a caper—and away he goes.

* * *

Life is fragile; handle with prayer.

* * *

Life is what happens while you're making other plans.

* * *

If life had a second edition, how would you correct the proofs?

* * *

Life is made up of sleeping, eating, working—and interruptions.

* * *

Life: A span of time of which the first half is ruined by your parents and the second half by your children.

What on earth will members of today's younger generation tell their children they had to do without?

*   *   *

For whoever finds me finds life and wins approval from the Lord (Proverbs 8:35).

*   *   *

All life is a school, a preparation, a purpose.

*   *   *

Many of us need the prayer of the old Scot, who mostly feared decay from the chin up: Lord, keep me alive while I'm still living.

*   *   *

Too many men conduct their lives on the cafeteria plan—self-service only.

*   *   *

As you walk down the fairway of life you must smell the roses, for you'll only get to play one round—*Ben Hogan*.

*   *   *

No matter what happens, there is always someone who knew it would.

Life is like tennis—a player who does not serve well often loses.

*   *   *

Life is like an ice-cream cone—you have to learn to lick it.

*   *   *

The greatest use of life is to spend it for something that will outlast it.

*   *   *

Taking life too seriously can make you a basket case.

*   *   *

Life is tragic for the person who has plenty to live on and nothing to live for—*Robert Fisk*.

*   *   *

Life is like one big labor dispute. It took only six days to create the world. The rest of the time men have been arguing about who was the Contractor.

*   *   *

Grass at eye-level is taller than the tall trees half a mile away.

Live one day at a time and make it a master-
piece.

*   *   *

Without a vision, the people perish (Proverbs 29:18
King James Version).

*   *   *

He who shoots at the sun will shoot higher than he
who aims at a tree.

*   *   *

Climb high, climb far; your aim the sky, your goal
the star.

*   *   *

Our plans miscarry because they have no aim.

*   *   *

When a man does not know what harbor he is
making for, no wind is the right wind.

Horizon Trail Mix

Faith is the daring of the soul to go farther than a distant horizon.

*   *   *

The amount of vision that dwells in a man is the correct measure of the man.

*   *   *

Personnel manager to applicant: What we're after is a man of vision; a man with drive, determination, fire; a man who never quits; a man who can inspire others; a man who can pull the company's bowling team out of last place!

*   *   *

At one time, a fellow with his ear to the ground was a politician. Now he's just somebody looking for a lost contact lens—*Vaughn Monroe*.

*   *   *

It doesn't hurt to dream as long as you get up and hustle when the alarm goes off.

You can never make your dreams come true by oversleeping.

*   *   *

If you love sleep, you'll end in poverty. Stay awake, work hard, and there will be plenty to eat! (Proverbs 20:13).

*   *   *

A person who is going nowhere can be sure of reaching his destination.

*   *   *

There's no point in carrying the ball until you learn where the goal is.

*   *   *

There's no sense aiming at a target with no arrow in your bow.

*   *   *

A teenager complained to a friend: My dad wants me to have all the things he never had when he was a boy—including five straight 'A's' on my report card.

*   *   *

He who kills time buries opportunities.

Do all the good you can,
By all the means you can,
In all the ways you can,
In all the places you can,
At all the times you can,
To all the people you can,
As long as ever you can.
—*John Wesley*

* * *

Find a goal for which you are willing to exchange a piece of your life.

* * *

Long-range goals keep you from being frustrated by short-termed failures.

* * *

There's something in life that never returns—a lost opportunity!

* * *

The reason a lot of people do not recognize opportunity is because it usually goes around wearing overalls looking like hard work.

* * *

The trouble with opportunity is that it's always more recognizable going than coming.

74

The older you get, the longer it takes to get to the door if opportunity knocks.

* * *

Opportunity knocks, but it has never been known to turn the knob and walk in.

* * *

Calvin Peete, a professional golfer who at 40 won more than $300,000 in 1982, after passing his high school equivalency test made this statement: Now that I am a high-school graduate, all kinds of opportunities should open up for me next year.

* * *

If you have an opportunity to do something worthwhile, don't talk about it but do it. After you have done it, your friends and enemies will talk about it.

* * *

Even if you're on the right track, you'll get run over if you just sit there—*Will Rogers*.

* * *

Do something! Either lead, follow, or get out of the way!

It is more important to know where you are going than to get there quickly.

*   *   *

Make hay while the sun shines—*English proverb*.

*   *   *

Do not mistake activity for achievement.

*   *   *

One ambitious boy's goal was this: to grow up and be a farmer so he can get paid for not raising spinach.

*   *   *

Why is it that all the vitamins are found in spinach rather than in ice cream?

Trix

Oh, what a tangled web we weave, when first we practice to deceive—*Sir Walter Scott*.

*   *   *

You can fool some of the people all of the time, and all of the people some of the time, but you cannot fool all of the people all of the time—*Abraham Lincoln*.

*   *   *

The greatest deceiver—he who deceives himself.

*   *   *

Self-deception is a short blanket—if you pull it over your face, you expose your feet.

*   *   *

Sometimes he who thinks he's in the groove is only in a rut.

Lord! Help! godly men are fast disappearing.
Where in all the world can dependable men be
found? Everyone deceives and flatters and lies.
There is no sincerity left (Psalm 12:1,2).

*　　*　　*

Disillusionment is what takes place when your son
asks you to help him with his algebra.

*　　*　　*

You could say a person wearing a toupee is living
under an assumed mane.

*　　*　　*

Rob: She said I'm interesting, brave, and
intelligent.

Bob: You should never go steady with a girl who
deceives you from the very start.

*　　*　　*

Never let a fool kiss you and never let a kiss fool
you.

*　　*　　*

You can fool some of the people all of the time,
and all of the people some of the time, but most of
the time they will make fools of themselves.

"Unhoney" Smack Attack

There's no such thing as idle rumors. They're always busy.

*   *   *

A rumor is about as hard to unspread as butter.

*   *   *

She has a bad case of rumortism.

*   *   *

It's easier to float a rumor than to sink one.

*   *   *

A tongue four inches long can kill a man six feet tall.

*   *   *

Some people will believe anything if you tell them it's a rumor.

If you must slander someone—don't speak it—but write it—write it in the sand, near the water's edge.

*   *   *

Slander, like coffee, is usually handed to you without grounds.

*   *   *

The slanderer differs from the assassin only in that he murders the reputation instead of the body.

*   *   *

Nothing is more frequently "opened by mistake" than the mouth.

*   *   *

A reputation takes years to build but only moments to destroy.

*   *   *

A good reputation is like a fortune, often harder to keep than to acquire.

*   *   *

No one raises his own reputation by lowering others.

The man who has to eat his own words never asks for a second helping.

*   *   *

Gossip is murder.

*   *   *

I try to watch the words I say,
    And keep them soft and sweet;
For I don't know from day to day,
    Which ones I'll have to eat.

*   *   *

So often the first screw that gets loose in a person's head is the one that holds the tongue in place.

*   *   *

People who plant a little gossip will reap a harvest of regret.

*   *   *

An evil man sows strife; gossip separates the best of friends (Proverbs 16:28).

*   *   *

Gossip always seems to travel fastest over grapevines that are slightly sour.

More people are run down by gossip than by automobiles.

*   *   *

He who throws dirt loses ground.

*   *   *

People who gossip usually wind up in their own mouthtraps.

*   *   *

A gossip is a person who will never tell a lie when the truth will do more damage.

*   *   *

If you are a liar, you had better have a good memory.

*   *   *

Abraham Lincoln said, "No man has a good enough memory to make a successful liar."

*   *   *

A lie will go around the world while truth is putting its boots on—*Dwight L. Moody*.

He who lies to himself in order to feel at ease is the worst sort of hypocrite.

* * *

Gossip is like soft soap—mostly lye!

* * *

A lie is a coward's way of getting out of trouble.

Proteen

No wonder it's tough for a teenager. Half the grown-ups tell him to find himself—the other half tell him to get lost!

*   *   *

A babysitter is a teenager who behaves like an adult, while the adults are out behaving like teenagers.

*   *   *

Teenage boys will drive anything—except a lawnmower.

*   *   *

Remember the good old days when a teenager went into the garage and came out with a lawnmower?

*   *   *

The trouble with teenagers is that if you ask them the number that comes after 9, they tell you it's Operator.

The only way you can have a heart-to-heart talk
with a teenager is to call her person-to-person.

*   *   *

A teenage girl reports that she's been trying to run
away from home for several months—but every
time she gets to the front door, the phone rings.

*   *   *

One mother's lament: "My teenage daughter is at
the stage where she's all skin and phones."

*   *   *

The father of a couple of teenagers called the
telephone company and announced, "I want to
report an obscene phone bill."

*   *   *

The main problem with teenagers is that they're
just like their parents were at their age.

*   *   *

The father was scolding his teenage daughter for
her slovenly appearance.

"You modern girls don't seem to care how you look
anymore," he declared. "Why, your hair looks like a
mop."

"What's a mop?" the daughter inquired innocently.

Father to son: Mind if I use the car tonight? I'm taking your mother out and I want to impress her.

* * *

Father to teenage son: No, you can't use the car— but please feel free to use the lawnmower.

* * *

One teenager to another: The trouble with father is that he remembers what it is to be young.

* * *

The accent may be on youth, but the stress is still on the parents.

* * *

Next year, 3½ million kids will turn 16, and 7 million parents will turn pale.

* * *

Really, the younger generation isn't so bad. It's just that they have more critics than models.

* * *

A teenager's aunt said she would like to buy him some records but wondered how to select them. So he wrote: "Listen to the beat, and if you don't like it, send it to me."

If you have teenagers in your household, you'll find it difficult to understand how farmers can possibly grow a surplus of food.

*   *   *

Teenagers are people who get hungry again before the dishes are even washed.

*   *   *

Home is a place where teenagers go to refuel.

*   *   *

Did you hear about the teenage boy who let his hair down—and smothered?

*   *   *

Having teenagers is often what undermines a parent's belief in heredity.

*   *   *

Parents of a teenage daughter are often miss-informed.

*   *   *

Going steady may be a matter of love, but for youngsters, it's merely Saturday night security.

Teenage love: A feeling you feel when you feel that what you feel is a feeling you have never felt before.

* * *

Teenager to doctor listening to her heart: Does it sound broken?

* * *

Rudy: I thought I told you not to tell Mom how late I came in last night.

Judy: I didn't tell her—I just told her I was too busy setting the breakfast table to notice the time.

* * *

Father to teenage daughter: I want you home by 11 o'clock.

Daughter: But Daddy, I am no longer a child!

Father: I know. That's why I want you home by 11.

* * *

Some young people think that curbing their emotions means parking by the roadside.

* * *

A generation crisis occurs when a teenager drives his car into the garage and runs over his father's bicycle.

A proud 16-year-old drove the car into the family driveway. His father sat beside him. Several younger brothers converged on the scene.

"I passed my driving test," shouted the happy driver. "You guys can all move up one bike."

*   *   *

"Just a trim," the teenage boy told the barber. "You can even it up a little around the shoulder."

*   *   *

Overheard at a teacher's meeting: I prefer to teach in an elementary school. I know I'll have a place to park my car there.

*   *   *

Old teachers never die, they just lose their principals.

Old principals never die, they just lose their faculties.

Old students never die, they just lose their class.

Sally was sobbing bitterly. Between sobs, she told the teacher, "I don't like school, and I have to stay here until I'm 16."

"Don't let that worry you," consoled the teacher. "I have to stay here till I'm 65."

*　　*　　*

Jim: You look all broken up. What's wrong?

Tim: I wrote home for money for a study lamp.

Jim: So what?

Tim: They sent the lamp!

*　　*　　*

Father to son, looking at his report card: Your grades don't promise much of a future, but your conduct marks indicate that you've already had quite a past!

*　　*　　*

Dad: Did you use the car last night?

Son: Yes, Dad. I took some of the boys for a ride.

Dad: Well, tell them I found two of their lipsticks.

Did you hear about the teenager who plans to run away from home just as soon as she gets a long enough telephone extension cord?

*　　*　　*

One thing that keeps a lot of youngsters from going to college is high school.

*　　*　　*

Sign on a high school bulletin board in Dallas: Free every Monday through Friday—Knowledge! Bring your own containers.

*　　*　　*

A teenager in Chicago played hookey from a correspondence school. He mailed in empty envelopes.

Product 19

Nineteen: the year when a youth is vacating his teens and tooling up for his twenties—usually as a freshman college student.

*   *   *

If all the people who live in college classes were laid end-to-end, they would be much more comfortable.

*   *   *

College professor: One who talks in other people's sleep.

*   *   *

You can lead a youth to college, but you cannot make him think.

*   *   *

College: A place to keep warm between high school and marriage.

College bred: A four-year loaf requiring a fearful amount of dough and seldom self-raising.

* * *

College years: The only vacation a boy gets between his mother and his wife.

* * *

One college freshman was so half-witted that he stayed up all night studying for a blood test.

* * *

Did you hear about the parents who were unable to afford a vacation because they had a son and daughter in college? They were suffering from "maltuition."

* * *

Our son in college is really a bright kid. He can think his way out of just about anything. He wrote across a very tough exam paper last December: "Only God knows the answers. Merry Christmas!"

He got his paper back, marked: "God gets an 'A'— you get an 'F.' Happy New Year!"

College education: A four-year plan for confusing a young mind methodically.

*   *   *

Sign on door of a college basketball coach's office: I'm busy, but if you can see over the transom, come in.

The Total Life

*Nineteen ingredients that help make
a productive, significant, and fulfilling life*

Attitude

It isn't your position that makes you happy or
unhappy; it's your disposition.

*   *   *

The greatest discovery of my generation is that
human beings can alter their lives by altering their
attitudes of mind—*William Jones*.

*   *   *

Two men look out through the same bars; one
sees the mud, the other sees the stars.

*   *   *

How does a man become wise? The first step is to
trust and reverence the Lord! Only fools refuse to
be taught. Listen to your father and mother. What
you learn from them will stand you in good stead;
it will gain you many honors (Proverbs 1:7-9).

The loser says: The worst is just around the corner.

The winner says: The best is yet to come.

*   *   *

Attitudes are more important than facts.

*   *   *

There is no danger of developing eye-strain from looking on the bright side of things.

Character

Character is what you are in the dark.

*   *   *

The measure of a man's character is what he would do if he knew he would never be found out—*Lord McCaulay.*

*   *   *

Good character, like good soup, is made at home.

*   *   *

A pat on the back develops character, if it is administered young enough, often enough, and low enough.

Character is what you really are; reputation is only what others believe you to be.

* * *

Character is much easier kept than recovered.

Commitment

Commitment in the face of conflict produces character.

* * *

Guidance means that I can count on God; commitment means that God can count on me.

* * *

Minister to the bride and groom: Do you, Tom and Valerie, promise, I mean really promise, I mean honest-to-goodness, solemnly, cross-your-heart-and-hope-to-die promise, not to go running off like spoiled brats to the divorce court after your first row?

* * *

Three kinds of people who lack commitment: cop-outs, drop-outs, and hold-outs.

* * *

For a commitment to be meaningful, it must result in mission.

Determination

Diamonds are chunks of coal that stuck to their job.

*   *   *

Some men succeed because they are destined to, but most men because they are determined to.

*   *   *

Some people grin and bear it. Others smile and change it.

*   *   *

The buck stops here—*Harry S. Truman.*

*   *   *

No man in the world has more determination than the one who can stop after eating one peanut.

*   *   *

Even the woodpecker owes his success to the fact that he uses his head and keeps pecking away until he finishes the job he started.

*   *   *

There is no greater champion than the man who conquers a bad habit.

*   *   *

One way to break a habit is to drop it.

Discipline

He who lives without discipline is exposed to grievous ruin—*Thomas à Kempis*.

* * *

Discipline yourself so others won't have to.

* * *

Self-discipline never means giving up anything—for giving up is a loss. Our Lord did not ask us to give up the things of earth, but to exchange them for better things—*Fulton J. Sheen*.

* * *

One sure way to test your willpower is to see a friend with a black eye and not ask any questions.

* * *

The undisciplined is a headache to himself and a heartache to others, and is unprepared to face the stern realities of life.

* * *

To live a disciplined life, and to accept the result of that discipline as the will of God—that is the mark of a man—*Tom Landry*.

Enthusiasm

Enthusiasm removes the gloom from the room.

What the world really needs is more people who will carry to their jobs the same enthusiasm for getting ahead as they display in traffic.

* * *

Enthusiasm is the best protection in any situation. Whole-heartedness is contagious.

* * *

A wise man once said that enthusiasm is nothing but faith with a tin can tied to its tail.

* * *

The fellow who is fired with enthusiasm for his work is seldom fired by his boss.

* * *

The gap between enthusiasm and indifference is filled with failures.

Faith

Faith is not a pill you swallow, but a muscle you use.

* * *

Sorrow looks back, worry looks around, but faith looks up.

Faith can rewrite your future.

*   *   *

It is impossible for faith to overdraw its account on the bank of heaven.

*   *   *

Pin your faith upon no man's sleeve. Have faith in God.

*   *   *

Feed your faith and your doubts will starve to death.

*   *   *

When faith goes to market, it always takes a basket.

*   *   *

He who prays for rain should carry an umbrella.

*   *   *

Faith hears the inaudible, sees the invisible, believes the incredible, and receives the impossible.

*   *   *

Faith is to the soul what a mainspring is to a watch.

Fear knocked at the door. Faith answered. No one was there.

*   *   *

When you can't figure out God's leading, don't falter—just faith it!

*   *   *

Church sign: Come in and have your faith lifted.

Friendship

Friendship doubles our joy and divides our grief.

*   *   *

He who seeks friends without faults stays forever without friends.

*   *   *

The best way to test a man's friendship is to ask him to co-sign your note. If he refuses, he is your friend.

*   *   *

It is poor judgment to countersign another's note, to become responsible for his debts (Proverbs 17:18).

The best way to wipe out a friendship is to sponge on it.

*   *   *

You're such a good friend—have you ever thought of turning pro?

*   *   *

He who knows all about you and still loves you just the same is a true friend.

*   *   *

Irish prayer: May the roof above us never fall in, and may we friends gathered below never fall out.

*   *   *

He who walks in when others walk out is a true friend.

*   *   *

You can always tell a real friend: When you've made a fool of yourself, he doesn't feel you've done a permanent job.

*   *   *

Be slow in choosing a friend, slower in changing—
Benjamin Franklin.

Probably the real reason the dog remains man's best friend is that neither borrows any money from the other.

* * *

The reason a dog is man's best friend is because he does not pretend—he proves it.

* * *

Always keep your head up—but be careful to keep your nose at a friendly level.

Gratitude

If you can't be thankful for what you receive, be thankful for what you escape.

* * *

Gratitude is the interest we owe God for the life He has loaned us.

* * *

During a railroad strike in England, a volunteer engineer on the London-Liverpool Express performed the remarkable feat of bringing the train into Liverpool 25 minutes ahead of time.

The passengers went forward in a body to thank him. A pale face emerged from the cab. "Don't thank me," he gasped, "thank God. I only found out how to stop this thing ten minutes ago!"

It's the second thank-you that proves you are grateful.

*   *   *

If you have a sore throat, be thankful you're not a giraffe.

*   *   *

He who forgets the language of gratitude can never be on speaking terms with happiness.

Hope

Life without hope is a life without meaning.

*   *   *

The best bridge between hope and despair is often a good night's sleep.

*   *   *

Probably nothing in the world arouses more false hopes than the first four hours of a diet—*Dan Bennett*.

*   *   *

Hope is what makes us live today as if tomorrow were yesterday.

*   *   *

He who has health has hope, and he who has hope has everything.

Never live in hope or expectation with your arms folded.

* * *

Lost hope is the undertaker's best friend.

* * *

Hope is faith holding out its hand in the dark.

* * *

Hope deferred makes the heart sick; but when dreams come true at last, there is life and joy (Proverbs 13:12).

* * *

There is hope for any man who can look in the mirror and laugh at what he sees.

Humor

Our five senses are incomplete without the sixth—a sense of humor.

* * *

Humor is the hole that lets the sawdust out of a stuffed shirt.

Humor is to life what shock absorbers are to automobiles.

*   *   *

On a school bulletin board: Laugh and the class laughs with you, but you stay after school alone!

*   *   *

Laughing is the sensation of feeling good all over and showing it principally in one spot—*Josh Billings*.

*   *   *

Laughter is the sun that drives winter from the human face—*Victor Hugo*.

*   *   *

> Give me a sense of humor, Lord;
> Give me the grace to see a joke,
> To get some happiness from life;
> And pass it on to other folk.

*   *   *

The best sense of humor belongs to the person who can laugh at himself.

*   *   *

Get-well cards have become so humorous that if you don't get sick you're missing a lot of fun.

Listening

We have two ears and only one tongue in order that
we may hear more and speak less—*Diogenes*.

* * *

A wise old owl lived in an oak;
The more he saw, the less he spoke;
The less he spoke, the more he heard;
Why can't we all be like that bird?

* * *

Every young man who listens to me and obeys my
instructions will be given wisdom and good sense
(Proverbs 2:1).

* * *

No man ever listened himself out of a job—*Calvin
Coolidge*.

* * *

Take a tip from nature—your ears aren't made to
shut, but your mouth is!

* * *

A winner listens, a loser can't wait until it's his turn
to talk.

Once a man learns how to listen, he and his wife can remain on speaking terms indefinitely.

Optimism

An optimist builds castles in the sky. A dreamer lives in them. A realist collects rent from both of them.

*   *   *

Keep your face to the sunshine and you cannot see the shadows—*Helen Keller*.

*   *   *

Optimistic bachelor: Let's get married!

Pessimistic spinster: Good heavens! Who'd have us!

*   *   *

An optimist is one who, instead of feeling sorry he cannot pay his bills, is glad he is not one of his creditors.

*   *   *

Optimism: A cheerful frame of mind that enables a tea kettle to sing though in hot water up to its nose.

*   *   *

An optimist is a man who, while waiting for a woman, keeps his motor running.

The optimist fell from the top story of a skyscraper. As he passed the tenth floor, he was overheard muttering: "So far, so good!"

*   *   *

The optimist is often as wrong as the pessimist; but he is far happier.

*   *   *

A few years ago, Montana State University had a bad football season, but the coach faced the new year optimistically. "We're sure to improve," he said. "We lost all ten games last season. This year we have only nine scheduled."

Perseverance

The thing to try when all else fails is again.

*   *   *

Giving it another try is better than an alibi.

*   *   *

The person who gets ahead is the one who does more than is necessary—and keeps on doing it.

*   *   *

He who really wants to do something finds a way; the other man finds an excuse.

Falling down doesn't make you a failure, but staying down does.

* * *

Failure is the path of least persistence.

* * *

Perseverance is the ability to stick to something you are not stuck on.

* * *

Many a man has failed because he had a wishbone where his backbone ought to have been.

Punctuality

The drawback of being punctual is that there's nobody there to appreciate it.

* * *

Nothing makes an office worker more punctual than 5 P.M.

* * *

Sign at the New Orleans airport: Start kissing good-bye early so the plane can leave on time.

* * *

Some folks never do anything on time except buy.

Punctuality is the virtue of kings—*German proverb*.

*   *   *

Punctuality is the politeness of princes.

*   *   *

Punctuality is the soul of business.

Respect

It is better to bind your children to you by respect and gentleness than by fear—*Terence*.

*   *   *

Respect every team—fear none.

*   *   *

One time when my friend was in the breeding business, he crossed a parrot with a tiger. He doesn't know what it is, but when it talks, everybody listens!

*   *   *

A child who is allowed to be disrespectful to his parents will not have true respect for anyone—*Billy Graham*.

*   *   *

He who respects his parents never dies.

Responsibility

"We are all responsible for our own sins," said the preacher. "It's no use trying to put the blame for them on someone else: Adam blamed Eve, Eve blamed the serpent, and the serpent didn't have a leg to stand on."

* * *

Sign on employee's desk: I have a very responsible job—when anything goes wrong, I'm responsible.

* * *

Man blames most accidents on fate—but feels personally responsible when he makes a hole-in-one on the golf course.

* * *

Some people grow under responsibility, while others only swell.

* * *

When you take responsibility on your shoulders, there is not much room left for chips.

Tact/Diplomacy

A man who remembers a woman's birthday but forgets her age is a diplomat.

Tact is the art of making guests feel at home when that's where you wish they were.

* * *

Tact is knowing how far to go before you go too far.

* * *

Tact is powdering your own no's.

* * *

Tact is the ability to close one's mouth before someone else wants to do it.

* * *

A diplomat is one who can bring home the bacon without spilling the beans.

* * *

Tact is the ability to give a person a shot in the arm without letting him feel the needle.

* * *

Tact is the knack of making a point without making an enemy.

If you want favor with both God and man, and a reputation for good judgment and common sense, then trust the Lord completely; don't ever trust yourself (Proverbs 3:4,5).

*   *   *

Tact is the ability to stay in the middle without getting caught there.

*   *   *

Diplomacy is the art of handling a porcupine without disturbing the quills.

Trust/Confidence

In God we trust—all others pay cash.

*   *   *

The men who trust God are the men that can be trusted.

*   *   *

When a train goes through a tunnel and it gets dark, you don't throw away your ticket and jump off. You sit still and trust the engineer—*Corrie ten Boom*.

The word "rely" is found only once in the Bible. We lie to God in our prayer when we don't rely on Him after our prayer.

*　　*　　*

If you trust God in the dark, He will change your "midnight" into music.

*　　*　　*

Look backward with gratitude and forward with confidence.

Instant Grits

Men occasionally stumble over the truth, but most of them pick themselves up and hurry off as if nothing had happened—*Winston Churchill*.

*   *   *

Truth does not hurt unless it ought to.

*   *   *

Those who stretch the truth usually find it snaps back.

*   *   *

A good thing about telling the truth is that you don't have to remember what you said.

*   *   *

If we could see ourselves
   As others see us,
We wouldn't even have
   The nerve to even be us.

Too often truth has only to change hands a few times to become fiction.

* * *

A man can't be always defending the truth; there must be a time to feed on it—*C. S. Lewis*.

* * *

Truth is stubborn. It doesn't apologize to anybody.

* * *

I don't want any yes-men around me. I want everyone to tell me the truth—even though it costs him his job—*Samuel Goldwin*.

* * *

Stretching the truth won't make it last any longer.

* * *

Truth is not always popular, but it is always right.

* * *

Men who never retract their opinions love themselves more than they love truth.

* * *

Beware of a half-truth; you may get hold of the wrong half.

The greatest homage we can pay to truth is to use it—*Emerson*.

* * *

A good man's mind is filled with honest thoughts; an evil man's mind is crammed with lies (Proverbs 12:5).

* * *

A tactful teacher sent this note home to all parents: If you promise not to believe everything your child says happens at school, I'll promise not to believe everything he says happens at home.

* * *

Grit: Courage; spirit; resolution.

* * *

Courage is fear that has said its prayers.

* * *

Why is it that no one wants to be brave anymore—just chief!

* * *

People who lack courage think with their legs.

It takes courage to stand up and speak, as well as to sit down and listen.

*   *   *

One person with courage makes a majority.

*   *   *

The wishbone will never replace the backbone—
Will Henry.

*   *   *

True courage is like a kite; a contrary wind forces it up, not down.

*   *   *

Don't be afraid to go out on a limb—that's where the fruit is!

*   *   *

Courage is the ability and determination to "hang in there" five minutes longer.

*   *   *

Courage is being the only one who knows you're afraid.

It's all right to be cautiously patient—but even a turtle never gets anywhere until he sticks his head out.

*   *   *

Actually, there's only a slight difference between keeping your chin up and sticking your neck out, but it's worth knowing.

*   *   *

Patience is the ability to count down before blasting off.

*   *   *

Make haste slowly and cautiously.

*   *   *

One who hurries, stumbles.

*   *   *

Patience is the thing you admire in the driver behind you and scorn in the one ahead.

*   *   *

Be patient when people growl at you—they may be living with a bear!

There are three rules for success: The first is to go on; the second is to go on; and the third is to go on.

*   *   *

The tree is not felled with one stroke.

*   *   *

Drop by drop the jug is filled.

*   *   *

The road to success is always under construction.

Alphabits of Wits

The best way to make your dreams come true is to wake up and get going.

*   *   *

You'll never make your dreams come true by over-sleeping.

*   *   *

We create our tomorrows by what we dream today.

*   *   *

He who is hungry dreams of bread, and he who thirsts, of springs.

*   *   *

Did you hear about the teenage girl who dreamed she ate a 5-pound marshmallow? When she woke up, her pillow was gone.

People who gaze at the stars are proverbially at the mercy of the puddles on the road.

*　　*　　*

Daydreaming: Wishcraft.

*　　*　　*

Intentions, like eggs, soon spoil unless hatched.

*　　*　　*

God provides the nuts, but He does not crack them.

*　　*　　*

Initiative is doing the right thing at the right time without being told.

*　　*　　*

People who have made a start have half the job done.

*　　*　　*

The more push a person possesses the less pull he needs. Every great man has been a self-starter.

The wise man looks ahead. The fool attempts to fool himself and won't face facts (Proverbs 14:8).

*   *   *

He who sits down cannot make footprints in the sands of time.

*   *   *

Work hard and become a leader; be lazy and never succeed (Proverbs 12:24).

*   *   *

Dreaming instead of doing is foolishness, and there is ruin in a flood of empty words; fear God instead (Ecclesiastes 5:7).

Life's Crunch

Crunch: A financial strain or cutback or stress of any kind.

*   *   *

One way to get stress is to go mountain climbing over molehills.

*   *   *

The Japanese business community calls pressure a 10,000-aspirin job.

*   *   *

Inflation is when the buck doesn't stop anymore.

*   *   *

Let our advance worrying become advance thinking and planning—*Winston Churchill.*

*   *   *

To carry worry to bed is like sleeping with a pack on your back.

Commit your work to the Lord, then it will succeed (Proverbs 16:3).

*   *   *

Nothing is so fatiguing as the eternal hanging-on of an uncompleted task—*William James*.

*   *   *

Our anxiety does not empty tomorrow of its sorrow, but only empties today of its strength— *Charles Spurgeon*.

*   *   *

Even a pro football coach faces stress. Not only does he have to be concerned about injuries to key players, but he has to worry about the cheerleaders getting pneumonia.

*   *   *

Don't grumble, don't bluster,
    don't dream and don't shirk.
Don't think of your worries,
    but think of your work.
The worries will vanish,
    the work will be done.
No man sees his shadow,
    who faces the sun.

Worry is like a rocking chair. It gives you
something to do but it doesn't get you any place.

*   *   *

One good reason for not worrying is that you feel
like a fool when things turn out all right.

Whole Grins for the Golden Years

You've reached middle-age when all you exercise is caution.

*   *   *

He who joins the health club but is too tired to drive there is probably middle-aged.

*   *   *

The trouble with middle-age is that you stop feeling your oats and start feeling your corn.

*   *   *

You know you're over the hill when you develop a taste for bran flakes.

*   *   *

He whose night-out is followed by a day-in is growing older.

Forty is the old age of youth, and fifty is the youth of old age.

*   *   *

You're over the hill when a night on the town is followed by two on your back.

*   *   *

You've just passed middle-age when the prospect of a good, short, midday nap is more enticing than that of a long night's sleep.

*   *   *

There's a new face cream for people over 40. It makes them look younger by giving them acne.

*   *   *

To me, old age is always 15 years older than I am— *Bernard Baruch*.

*   *   *

Age is a question of mind over matter. If you don't mind, it doesn't matter—*Satchel Paige*.

*   *   *

The trouble with life is that by the time a fellow gets to be an old hand at the game, he starts losing his grip.

A young reporter asked a stylish, vibrant, elderly woman if she'd mind telling her age. "Not at all," she replied. "I'm plenty-nine."

* * *

When you're over the hill, your speed picks up.

* * *

I don't intend to grow old gracefully—I'm fighting every inch of the way.

* * *

The three ages of man: one, youth; two, middle-age; and three, "My, you look good!"

* * *

"I've been going with your daughter for 15 years now," said the bashful gentleman to her father. "Would you object if we got married?"

"Certainly not," said the relieved father. "I was afraid you were going to ask for a pension."

* * *

Old minds are like old horses; you must exercise them if you wish to keep them in working order— *John Adams*.

Life gets more enjoyable the older you get. The hardest years in life are between 10 and 70—*Helen Hayes*.

*   *   *

If you want to know how old a woman is, ask her sister-in-law.

*   *   *

The principal objection to old age is there is no future in it.

*   *   *

Violinist Mischa Elman began his concert career when he was a boy. Listeners would say in wonder, "Isn't it amazing what he can do at his age?"

When he reached 70, nothing was changed. Listeners still said in wonder, "Isn't it amazing what he can do at his age?"

*   *   *

One cannot help being old—but one can resist being aged.

*   *   *

You may be sure your youth has fled when you precede your kids to bed.

You're an old-timer if you remember when castor oil and camphor were the miracle drugs.

*　　*　　*

There are three things that grow more precious with age: old wood to burn, old books to read, and old friends to enjoy.

*　　*　　*

I will be your God through all your lifetime, yes, even when your hair is white with age. I made you and I will care for you. I will carry you along and be your Savior (Isaiah 46:4).

*　　*　　*

There's many a good tune in an old fiddle!

Granola Snacks and Smacks

Common sense, also known as horse sense, is the sixth sense (though not as common as it used to be), given to us by God to keep the other five from making fools of themselves—and us.

*   *   *

The man who strays away from common sense will end up dead! (Proverbs 21:16).

*   *   *

This country is where it is today on account of the real common sense of the normal majority—*Will Rogers*.

*   *   *

Common sense is seeing things as they are, and doing things as they should be done.

*   *   *

Horse sense is stable thinking coupled with the ability to say "nay."

Wisdom and good judgment live together, for wisdom knows where to discover knowledge and understanding. If anyone respects and fears God, he will hate evil. For wisdom hates pride, arrogance, corruption and deceit of every kind (Proverbs 8:12,13).

* * *

Horse sense shows itself when a fellow knows enough to stay away from a nag.

* * *

Horse: An oatsmobile.

* * *

One way to stop a runaway horse is to bet on him.

* * *

A horse can't pull while kicking,
    This fact I merely mention;
And he can't kick while pulling,
    Which is my chief contention.

Let's imitate the good old horse,
    And lead a life that's fitting;
Just pull an honest load, and then
    There'll be no time for kicking.

Get the facts at any price, and hold on tightly to all the good sense you can get (Proverbs 23:23).

*   *   *

Horse sense dwells in a stable mind.

*   *   *

It is a thousand times better to have common sense without intelligence than to have intelligence without common sense.

*   *   *

Determination to be wise is the first step toward becoming wise! And with your wisdom, develop common sense and good judgment (Proverbs 4:7).

*   *   *

He who wants to be outstanding in his field must be willing to use horse sense.

*   *   *

A Shetland pony is nothing but a compact horse.

*   *   *

A racehorse is an animal that can take several thousand people for a ride at the same time.

In the good old days, a horse had sense enough to take a second look at a railroad crossing.

* * *

Not only is the horse just about extinct, but so are the people who work like one.

* * *

A bad combination: three hundred horsepower under the hood and no horse sense behind the wheel.

* * *

Beta (at riding academy): I wish to rent a horse.

Groomer: How long?

Beta: The longest you've got. There will be five of us going.

* * *

It takes a lot of horse sense to maintain a stable government.

* * *

Snap judgments would be all right if they didn't come unsnapped so often.

* * *

If you must go against your better judgment, do it when *she's* not around!

The best some of us can expect on the Day of
Judgment is a suspended sentence.

*   *   *

Before you pass judgment on a sermon, be sure to
try it out and practice it first.

*   *   *

Never judge a man's action until you know his
motives.

*   *   *

It's easy to miscalculate the actions and words of
those we dislike.

*   *   *

The best way to judge a man is not by what other
men say about him, but by what he says about other
men.

*   *   *

Don't judge your friend until you stand in his
place.

*   *   *

In judging others it's always wise to see with the
heart as well as with the eyes.

If for a tranquil mind you seek,
　These things observe with care:
Of whom you speak, to whom you speak
　And how, and when, and where.

Krispie Kritters

Fun animal quips from A to Zoo

A rabbit is not supposed to climb trees, but sometimes he must.

*   *   *

It's not so much the size of the dog in the fight that counts, but the size of the fight in the dog.

*   *   *

A dog is loved by old and young; he wags his tail and not his tongue.

*   *   *

He who growls all day, lives a dog's life.

*   *   *

He who lies down with the dogs will get up with the fleas.

*   *   *

He who wants to trick the fox must rise early.

A man who hunts two hares leaves one and loses the other.

* * *

He who wants to soar with the eagles must avoid running with turkeys.

* * *

People who want eggs must endure cackling hens.

* * *

Human beings, like chickens, thrive best when they scratch for what they get.

* * *

Nothing will cook your goose faster than a red-hot temper.

* * *

A mule makes no headway when he's kicking— neither does a man.

* * *

Sign on Australian kangaroo farm: Our kangaroos grow by leaps and bounds.

* * *

Nothing in the world is friendlier than a wet dog.

Did you hear about the clever cat who ate some cheese and breathed down the rat hole with bated breath?

*　　*　　*

Two kangaroos were talking to each other and one said, "I hope it doesn't rain today. I just hate it when the kids play inside."

*　　*　　*

The hippopotamus was next to the giraffe in the zoo. The giraffe peered over the fence and said to the hippo, "Boy, I sure feel lousy. I have a sore throat. It's killing me!"

The hippo exclaimed, "You think you've got troubles! I have chapped lips."

*　　*　　*

Carrots are definitely good for the eyes. Have you ever seen a rabbit with glasses?

*　　*　　*

It's nice for children to have pets until the pets start having children.

*　　*　　*

The reason the cow jumped over the moon was because there was a short circuit in the milking machine.

A scientist recently crossed a carrier pigeon with a woodpecker. The bird not only carries messages, but he knocks on the door.

*   *   *

Bob: Don't be afraid of my dog. You know the old proverb, "A barking dog never bites."

Rich: Yes, you know the proverb, and I know the proverb, but does your dog know the proverb?

*   *   *

Mother rabbit to her little bunny: A magician pulled you out of a hat . . . now stop asking questions.

*   *   *

Fran: What do you call ten angry dolphins?

Stan: Cross-porpoises.

*   *   *

Did you hear what the mother hen said to the scrambled eggs? "Dig those crazy mixed-up kids!"

*   *   *

If you have occasion to criticize a mule, do it to his face.

The panther is like a leopard,
  Except it hasn't been peppered.
Should you behold a panther crouch,
  Prepare to say "ouch."
Better yet, if called by a panther,
  Don't anther.

—Ogden Nash

Corn Pops

A baby's cry in the night has great carrying power, and Dad is generally the carrier.

*   *   *

A proud father phoned the newspaper and reported the birth of twins. The girl at the desk didn't quite catch the message.

"Will you repeat that?" she asked.

"Not if I can help it," he replied.

*   *   *

Smart son: Dad, I just siphoned a couple of gallons of gas out of your car for my old bus. It's okay, isn't it?

Smarter father: Sure, it's okay, son. I bought that gas with your allowance for next week. So run along and have a good time.

*   *   *

A father is a banker provided by nature.

Father: When George Washington was your age, son, he was a surveyor.

Son: And when he was your age, Dad, he was president.

*　　*　　*

Father: A kin you love to touch.

*　　*　　*

It's the running expenses that keep fathers out of breath.

*　　*　　*

Fathers give daughters away to other men who aren't good enough . . . so they can have grandchildren that are smarter than anybody else's.

*　　*　　*

The father of a motherless young girl was giving instructions before his daughter's first date: Just follow the directions on your mayonnaise jar.

She read it: Keep cool, but do not freeze.

*　　*　　*

One father is worth more than a hundred school-masters.

The head of the American family should speak in a loud, firm voice—and she does!

*   *   *

The sentiments expressed by the man of the house are not necessarily those of the management.

*   *   *

What the average man wants to get out of his new car is the kids.

*   *   *

A father is a person who spends thousands of dollars on his daughter's wedding and then reads in the paper that he gave her away.

*   *   *

Teenage daughter, introducing her date to her father: Egbert, meet my answering service.

*   *   *

When my father found me on the wrong track, he always provided switching facilities.

*   *   *

Young father discussing baby: We just can't go anywhere—he's such a wet blanket.

A diplomat is a father with two boys on different Little League teams.

* * *

A graduate student who is majoring in child psychology developed a lecture on "The Ten Commandments for Parents." When he married and became a father, he altered the title to "Ten Hints for Parents."

Another child arrived and he then lectured on "Some Suggestions for Parents."

When the third child arrived, he stopped lecturing!

* * *

Education is something you get when your father sends you to college, but it isn't complete until you send your own son.

* * *

The most important thing a father can do for his children is to love their mother.

* * *

A real family man is one who looks at his new child as an addition rather than a deduction.

Nowadays, a father can remember his son's first haircut—but not his last.

* * *

Fathers of college students get poorer by degrees.

* * *

Friend: What were your father's last words?

Daughter: He didn't have any. Mother was with him to the end.

* * *

The trouble with being a father is that by the time you're experienced, you're unemployable.

* * *

A father is forced to endure childbirth without an anesthetic.

* * *

A boy's best friend is his father, and if he gets up early and stays up late, he may get to see him.

* * *

When I was a boy of 14, my father was so ignorant I could hardly stand to have the old man around. But when I got to be 21, I was astonished at how much he had learned in 7 years—*Mark Twain*.

Thoughtful father: If my son is getting as much out of college as his college is getting out of me, he will be a success.

*   *   *

A wise son makes a glad father (Proverbs 10:1 Revised Standard Version).

*   *   *

Father of a Harvard undergraduate, bragging: My son's letters always send me to the dictionary!

Dad two: You're lucky. My son's letters always send me to the bank.

*   *   *

Officer (to man pacing sidewalk at 3 o'clock in the morning): What are you doing here?

Gentleman: I forgot my key, officer, and I'm waiting for my children to come home and let me in.

Creamed Wit

When you get to wit's-end corner, keep your wits about you.

*   *   *

When frustration takes over and you get to the end of your rope, tie a knot and hang on.

*   *   *

Did you hear about the frustrated child who remembered asking her mother where she came from . . . and her mother gave her a phony address in Seattle?

*   *   *

First clerk: What a frustrating day! I sold only one dress yesterday, and today is even worse.

Second clerk: How could it be worse?

First clerk: Today the lady returned the dress she bought yesterday!

Don't throw away the old bucket until you know whether the new one holds water—*Swedish proverb*.

* * *

Futility: Cleaning your house while your kids are still growing is like shoveling the walk before it stops snowing.

* * *

No man ever gets very far pacing the floor.

* * *

Customers who ask the waiter for a piece of meat without fat, gristle, or bones should order eggs.

* * *

Stand firm for what you know is right,
    It's wise, as I have found.
The mighty oak was once a nut,
    That simply held its ground.

* * *

The last key in the bunch is often the one that opens the lock.

* * *

Perseverance is not a long race; it is many short races one after another—*Walter Elliott*.

By perseverance the snail reached the Ark—*Charles Spurgeon*.

* * *

Never give up, and never give in—*Hubert Humphrey*.

* * *

By gnawing through a dike, even a rat may drown a nation—*Edmund Burke*.

* * *

Little strokes fell great oaks—*Benjamin Franklin*.

* * *

Fall seven times, stand up eight—*Japanese proverb*.

* * *

The falling drops at last will wear the stone—*Lucretius*.

* * *

> The ones we are saluting,
>   Are not so highfaluting.
> The very big shots,
>   Are the little shots,
> Who only kept on shooting.

Fruit and Fiber of Living

God never wastes a furrow; He plows in your life in order to produce fruit from your life.

*   *   *

If you want the fruit, you must climb the tree.

*   *   *

People who eat forbidden fruit will end up in a jam.

*   *   *

Men who plant fruit trees love others besides themselves.

*   *   *

If you want to enjoy the fruit, you must not pick the blossoms. (Don't sacrifice tomorrow on the altar of today.)

*   *   *

Deeds are fruits; words are leaves.

By their fruits, you will know them (Matthew 7:20 New King James Version).

*   *   *

Those who plant walnut trees do not expect to eat the fruit.

*   *   *

Adam ate the apple, and our teeth still ache—
Hungarian proverb.

*   *   *

It wasn't the apple on the tree, but the pair on the ground that caused so much trouble in the Garden of Eden.

*   *   *

Adam was created first—to give him a chance to say something.

*   *   *

Teacher: Why was Adam a famous runner?

Student: Because he was first in the human race.

*   *   *

Adam really had a good thing going—when he said something, he knew nobody had said it before.

Adam may have had his troubles, but at least he didn't have to listen to Eve talking about the man she could have married.

*   *   *

Eve: Adam, do you love me?

Adam: Who else?

*   *   *

Eve was the first person to eat herself out of house and home.

*   *   *

Failure is a better teacher than success, but she seldom finds an apple on her desk.

*   *   *

Sal: What is sweet, has custard, and is bad-tempered?

Al: Apple Grumble.

*   *   *

You can't get the worm out of the apple by polishing the apple.

*   *   *

Timely advice is as lovely as golden apples in a silver basket (Proverbs 25:11).

Stones and sticks are thrown only at fruit-bearing trees.

*   *   *

Adam was rejected for Eden the apple.

*   *   *

An apple a day keeps the doctor away.

*   *   *

A pear must be eaten to the day; if you don't eat it then, throw it away!

*   *   *

A man who thinks he can find some big strawberries at the bottom of the box is an optimist.

*   *   *

Question: What did Adam and Eve do when they were expelled from the Garden?

Answer: They started raisin' Cain.

Rocky Road

When the going gets tough, the tough get going—
Robert Schuller.

* * *

It is a rough road that leads to the heights of
greatness—*Seneca.*

* * *

All roads to success are uphill.

* * *

Gold is tried by fire, brave men by adversity—
Seneca.

* * *

Adversity: the only diet that will reduce a fat head.

* * *

Adversity introduces a man to himself.

You are a poor specimen if you can't stand the pressure of adversity.

*   *   *

The darker the day, the more we must pray.

*   *   *

If you want a place in the sun, you have to expect some blisters.

*   *   *

Adversity tries great men; prosperity the small ones.

*   *   *

After crosses and losses, men grow humbler and wiser—*Benjamin Franklin*.

*   *   *

Adversity causes some men to break, others to break records.

*   *   *

When everything seems to be going against you, remember that the airplane takes off against the wind, not with it.

It's easy enough to be pleasant,
    When everything goes like a song;
But the man worthwhile,
    Is the man who can smile,
When everything seems to go wrong.

* * *

A smooth sea never made a skillful mariner.

* * *

Adversity makes men think of God—*Livy*.

* * *

Graduation from the University of Adversity will help prepare you for a life of diversity.

* * *

The brook would lose its song if we removed the rocks.

* * *

In time of prosperity,
    Friends will be plenty;
In time of adversity,
    Not one in twenty.

* * *

When trouble moves in, make it pay rent.

People who gather roses should not be alarmed by the thorns.

*   *   *

If you could kick the person responsible for most of your troubles, you wouldn't be able to sit down for six months.

*   *   *

The best way to meet trouble is to face it.

*   *   *

Today's troubles are so often yesterday's unsolved problems.

*   *   *

With me, a change of trouble is as a vacation—*David Lloyd George*.

*   *   *

When the shepherd speaks well of the wolf, the sheep are in trouble.

*   *   *

The trouble with being a breadwinner nowadays is that the government is in for such a big slice—*Mary McCoy*.

*   *   *

Troubles are like babies—they only grow if you nurse them.

The only fellow whose troubles are all behind him is a school-bus driver.

* * *

A lot of our troubles are caused by too much bone in the head and not enough in the back.

* * *

It's strange how trouble always starts out as being fun.

* * *

If nobody knows the trouble you've seen, you don't live in a small town.

* * *

Half the troubles of this life can be traced to saying yes too quickly and not saying no soon enough— *Josh Billings*.

* * *

The real test in golf and in life is not keeping out of the rough, but in getting out after we are in— *John Moore*.

* * *

A steep grade separates the men from the boys.

A dog, following his master's car, saw a cat, paused momentarily, then kept going. Every man has a cat—temptation.

*   *   *

The True Test

Does he miss church service?
  He *may* be sick.
Does he miss work?
  He *probably* is sick.
Does he miss his favorite sport
or amusement?
  He is *really* sick!

*   *   *

A testimony is what's left after the test.

*   *   *

A good skipper proves himself during a storm.

*   *   *

You are not tempted because you are evil; you are tempted because you are human.

*   *   *

What makes resisting temptation difficult, for many people, is that they don't want to discourage it completely.

The diamond cannot be polished without friction, nor man perfected without trials.

* * *

When a man feels sure he is free from temptation, it's a sure sign he should be on his guard.

* * *

Take two coins that look exactly alike. One is genuine, the other is counterfeit. How can you tell them apart? The secret service men tell us we should throw them on a table. The coin that doesn't bounce is counterfeit. The coin that bounces is the real thing.

Life tests men in the same way—by their bounce! The men who do not possess real worth, quit. The men of value bounce. Lincoln was defeated many times, yet always bounced back and finally bounced into the White House. Edison failed many times in his effort to invent the incandescent lamp, yet he always bounced back and tried again—and finally he won. In the Hall of Accomplishment, you'll find inscribed the names of the men and women who bounced.

* * *

Opportunity knocks, but temptation kicks the door down. Opportunity knocks only once; temptation leans on the doorbell.

The devil tempts all men; but the idle man tempts the devil.

*   *   *

When you meet temptation, turn to the right.

*   *   *

There's a sure-fire method of withstanding the temptation to go overboard with credit cards. It's called plastic surgery—*Burt Murray.*

*   *   *

When you flee from temptation, be sure you don't leave a forwarding address.

*   *   *

A driver tucked this note under the windshield wiper of his automobile: I've circled the block for 20 minutes. I'm late for an appointment and if I don't park here, I'll lose my job. Forgive us our trespasses.

When he came back, he found a parking ticket and this note: I've circled the block for 20 years, and if I don't give you a ticket, I'll lose my job. Lead us not into temptation.

*   *   *

Eternal vigilance is the price of liberty.

Upon the fields of friendly strife, are sown the
seeds that, upon other fields, on other days, will
bear the fruits of victory—*Douglas MacArthur*.

*   *   *

Unless there is within us that which is above us, we
will soon yield to that which is around us.

Frosted Mini-Wits

Bachelor: One who treats all women as sequels.

*   *   *

Calories: Weight lifters.

*   *   *

Flattery: The applause that refreshes.

*   *   *

Forger: The man who gives a check a bad name.

*   *   *

Marriage: Love parsonified.

*   *   *

Maybe: The preamble to hope.

*   *   *

Mummies: Egyptians pressed for time.

Professional men: Slaves to conventions.

* * *

Rare volume: A returned book.

* * *

Sarcasm: Barbed ire.

* * *

Yes: A married woman's last word.

* * *

Yawn: A silent shout.

* * *

Baby: Mommy's little yelper.

* * *

Credit card: The sweet buy and buy.

* * *

Dieting: A matter of mind over platter.

* * *

Egotist: An "I" specialist.

Fat: The penalty for exceeding the feed limit.

*   *   *

Gossip: Ear pollution.

*   *   *

Hangover: The moaning after the night before.

*   *   *

Hug: A roundabout way of expressing affection.

*   *   *

Inflation: A drop in the buck.

*   *   *

Kiss: Nothing divided by two.

*   *   *

Love: Emotion in motion.

*   *   *

Mud: Mud thrown is ground lost.

*   *   *

Sneezing: Much "achoo" about nothing.

Sympathy: Thinking with your heart.

* * *

Tomorrow: The graveyard of great possibilities.

* * *

Twins: Infant replay.

* * *

Violinist: One who is up to his chin in music.

* * *

Motel sign: Inn-Mates Wanted.

* * *

Bakery sign: We discovered our roll in life.

* * *

Alimony: The high cost of leaving.

* * *

Angel: A pedestrian who forgot to jump.

* * *

Beatnik: Santa Claus the day after Christmas.

Busybody: One who burns a "scandle" at both ends.

*   *   *

Prune: A plum who has seen better days.

*   *   *

Used car: A car in first-crash condition.

*   *   *

Desk: A wastebasket with drawers.

*   *   *

Doghouse: Mutt hut.

*   *   *

Flu season: Hoarse and buggy days.

*   *   *

Free thinker: One who is not married.

*   *   *

Giving: The hardest thing to give is in.

*   *   *

Haste: Hasty climbers have sudden falls.

In-laws: Advice Squad.

* * *

Laughter: He who laughs—lasts.

* * *

Belly laugh: Mirthquake.

* * *

Laziness: The mother of intention.

* * *

Politics: The most promising of all careers.

* * *

Puppy love: The beginning of a dog's life.

* * *

Restaurant chains: Cook-alikes.

* * *

Sarcasm: Quiplash.

* * *

Triumph: "Umph" added to try.

* * *

Work: The yeast that raises the dough.

Cheerios
Final Last Bites

Down the street his funeral goes,
    As sobs and wails diminish.
He died through drinking varnish,
    But he had a lovely finish.

*   *   *

Today is the first day of the rest of your life. Live it as if it were going to be your last!

*   *   *

The greatest thing in the world is not so much where you stand, as in what direction you are moving.

*   *   *

Where you go hereafter depends on *what* you go after here.

*   *   *

The most frustrating occupation in the world must be an elevator operator. She never gets to hear the end of a good story.

There are some things in this world you can count on. For example, you'll never see a television commercial with an unhappy ending—*Robert Orben*.

* * *

Scene in the high school chemistry class:

Boy: Au revoir!
Girl: What's that?
Boy: That's good-bye in French.
Girl: Carbolic acid!
Boy: What's that?
Girl: Good-bye in *any* language!

* * *

You fall the way you lean.

* * *

Wealthy people miss one of life's greatest pleasures—paying the last installment.

* * *

If you only knock long enough and loud enough at the gate, you are sure to wake up somebody—*Henry W. Longfellow*.

* * *

George Washington fought nine major battles in the Revolutionary War. He lost six of these battles, but won the war!

183

Be like a postage stamp: Stick to one thing until
you get there.

*　　*　　*

Sunday's coming—hang in there!

*　　*　　*

Prayer: Lord, give us the tenacity and
determination of a weed.

*　　*　　*

Persistent people begin their success where others
end in failure.

*　　*　　*

Bite off more than you can chew,
　　then chew it.
Plan more than you can do,
　　then do it.
Point your arrow at a star,
　　take your aim, and there you are.

Arrange more time than you can spare,
　　then spare it.
Take on more than you can bear,
　　then bear it.
Plan your castle in the air,
　　then build a ship to take you there.

An optimist is anyone who reaches for the car keys in his pocket when an after-dinner speaker says, "In conclusion . . ."

* * *

In conclusion: The phrase that wakes up the audience.

* * *

People who jump to conclusions usually make a very bad landing.

* * *

The sermon went on and on and on in the hot church. At last the minister paused and asked, "What more, my friend, can I say?"

In the back of the church a voice offered earnestly, "Amen!"

* * *

So be it!

Index

186

188

More
Harvest House Books
by *Vern McLellan*

PROVERBS FOR PEOPLE

Clever, provocative proverbs are matched with a corresponding Bible reference and illustration that will bring a smile and a cause for reflection with the turn of each page. Here's a sample: Proverb: He who gossips usually winds up in his own mouthtrap. Proverbs 16:28: An evil man sows strife; gossip separates the best of friends.

QUIPS, QUOTES, AND QUESTS

You'll never be without a wise or witty saying after you read *Quips, Quotes, and Quests*. This inspiring collection of 1,098 famous (and infamous) quotations, Bible verses, and common sense sayings is a handy reference book for the whole family. If you like stimulating, insightful one-liners, this is the book for you.

PROVERBS, PROMISES, AND PRINCIPLES

This inspiring book is jammed with penetrating insights and poignant points that will add exciting new dimensions to your life and conversation. If you're a teacher, preacher, writer, researcher, parent or student, you'll find humorous, practical proverbs, timely Bible promises, and powerful principles to apply to living.

Other Good
Harvest House Reading

THE ALL AMERICAN JOKE BOOK
by *Bob Phillips*

A riotous, fun-filled collection of over 800 anecdotes, puns, and jokes.

BIBLE FUN
by *Bob Phillips*

Jam-packed full of brain-teasing crossword puzzles, intricate mazes, word jumbles, and other mind benders. *Bible Fun* will keep you occupied for hours—with the added bonus of honing your Bible knowledge. Sharpen your pencil and put your thinking cap on—you're about to be a-maze-d!

THE LAST OF THE GOOD CLEAN JOKES
by *Bob Phillips*

The master joker edits and arranges wisecracks, rib ticklers, and zany puns.

MORE GOOD CLEAN JOKES
by *Bob Phillips*

An entertaining fun-book designed for public speakers, pastors, and everyone who enjoys good clean jokes.

THE RETURN OF THE GOOD CLEAN JOKES
by *Bob Phillips*
Over 900 quips, anecdotes, gags, puns, and wisecracks.

Dear Reader:

We would appreciate hearing from you regarding this Harvest House nonfiction book. It will enable us to continue to give you the best in Christian publishing.

1. What most influenced you to purchase *Shredded Wit*?
   - ☐ Author
   - ☐ Subject matter
   - ☐ Backcover copy
   - ☐ Recommendations
   - ☐ Cover/Title
   - ☐ _____

2. Where did you purchase this book?
   - ☐ Christian bookstore
   - ☐ General bookstore
   - ☐ Other
   - ☐ Grocery store
   - ☐ Department store

3. Your overall rating of this book:
   - ☐ Excellent   ☐ Very good   ☐ Good
   - ☐ Fair   ☐ Poor

4. How likely would you be to purchase other books by this author?
   - ☐ Very likely
   - ☐ Somewhat likely
   - ☐ Not very likely
   - ☐ Not at all

5. What types of books most interest you? (check all that apply)
   - ☐ Women's Books
   - ☐ Marriage Books
   - ☐ Current Issues
   - ☐ Self Help/Psychology
   - ☐ Bible Studies
   - ☐ Fiction
   - ☐ Biographies
   - ☐ Children's Books
   - ☐ Youth Books
   - ☐ Other _____

6. Please check the box next to your age group.
   - ☐ Under 18   ☐ 25-34   ☐ 45-54
   - ☐ 18-24   ☐ 35-44   ☐ 55 and over

Mail to: Editorial Director
Harvest House Publishers
1075 Arrowsmith
Eugene, OR 97402

Name _____

Address _____

City _____ State _____ Zip _____